SOFTER

MARIA K CRAWFORD

SOFTER

MARIA K CRAWFORD

Softer Copyright © 2021 by Maria K Crawford.

All rights reserved.

ISBN: 978-0-578-88240-6

Maria K Crawford

www.mariakcrawford.com

Cover design by Align Design Co.

Author photo by Lauren Kennedy

SOFTER

Dedication

This one is for me.

MARIA K CRAWFORD

SOFTER

To my reader

Just promise, no matter what,

You'll keep going.

Just keep going.

SOFTER

Maybe I will rise from ashes
You did more than burn me out

MARIA K CRAWFORD

SOFTER

Thanks to you

I want to go on thinking

That I didn't run from something good

Into the devil's arms

But I ran to you

Like gasoline up the slender curve of a flame

That's ok—

I don't think I'd be here

About to buy bohemian rugs

For an apartment I'd host parties in

If you hadn't played with me

The way the devil plays with temptation

So, I'm glad you made me sick

Now I can feel joy

So marvelously

Without you

After you

In the absence of you

I mean, think about it

Even music sounds so much more fucking beautiful

Since I learned a whole new meaning

Of

Ugly

Thanks to you

You can't keep them
You can't keep them
You can't keep them

If there were ever a voice in my head

It would be that one

I don't want to keep them

Until I do

And then never strikes me

Like I imagine lightning strikes

The prettiest trees

SOFTER

It's always been

You

And I can't say

How bad a thing

That is for

Me

I remember the feeling

Wanting to wash you away

The dirt still on my skin

Now in layers

If I had only let the water run over me

All that time ago

The drain would have been circled in brown

Only for a moment

But it will take time now

To wash you away

You might not ever be untraceable

After all the garbage

You've covered me in

SOFTER

I realized I wasn't making coffee

Because you aren't here

And most of the times I made it

Ended in me handing a carefully chosen mug your way

It was one thing you always said thank you for

But I made coffee today

And I think I'll start eating again

I almost walked to Tandem this morning

Just trying to fill the void of sitting in our kitchen alone

I realized as I listened to the shitty coffee maker rumble

I was more in love with choosing the mug

And hearing you thank me

Than I was with you

At the end

I wonder if my next lover will like decaf

My pretty little apartment

Is starting to feel like

A pretty little prison

The walls getting tighter every day

When I think of you

Being here

SOFTER

I sit and think about the things I like about it here

How seagulls fly over pale yellow houses

And how it smells like the sea

Even in the winter

If you're on the right street

God, I wonder if you'll ever get better

And see it, too

It's not about that right now

Unsure lovers

Anxious hummingbirds

Speckled noses from cigarette ash and mascara

Talking about when you were happy before

Anxious hummingbirds

Pulling teeth in conversation

Talking about when you were happy before

Your lover becomes your friend

Pulling teeth in conversation

Phone calls from your mother

Your lover becomes your friend

Regret creeps in

Phone calls from your mother

She asks you if you're ok

Regret creeps in

You wonder if you're still in love

She asks you if you're ok

This time in your kitchen

You wonder if you're still in love

It's not about that right now

SOFTER

This time in your kitchen

You remember you aren't eating

It's not about that right now

When was the last time you felt like yourself?

It's hard not to think about

Speckled noses from cigarette ash and mascara

It's true that you cried when you kissed him on the face

Unsure lovers

I sat

Organizing love poems I wrote about you

Over the course of a year

Listening to French music

Imagining we lived in Paris

While you

Flirted with another girl

In your cubicle

SOFTER

You liked the way

My hair looks

Curled

But you like her hair that way

Better

Harrowing home

Humble havoc

Happiness fleeting

I hobble down the habitual path

Honey dripping from my half-assed wishes

Hoping for hunger to help me try again

I'm left hanging

Hunting for heaven

Nothing but horrible habits haunting me

The heater cries

Hums at me

It's happy hour,

It hisses

I'm hunched over

I'm sure hell exists

I hate of all this

SOFTER

I haven't written

Frozen in any attempt to feel comfortable

Even my fingertips need rest

After you

It's only 5:30

And it scares me when time starts to feel

Endless

It's only 5:30

And

That's too early

Because

Sleeping is the only way out

Right now

It's only 5:30

And no matter what I do

Or how I cry

Everyone leaves

And

No one stays

It's only 5:30

And that means

I have a whole night ahead of me

To feel this way

It's only 5:30

And

It's one more day

I'm nauseas

Over you

It's only 5:30

SOFTER

All I can do now

Is pray

And that's something

I normally wouldn't do

But here I am

Praying

That this feeling

In the bottom of my heart

In the pit of my stomach

At the root of my mind

That I'll be safe

And loved

Is real

And on its way to me

From somewhere beautiful

To greet me

And never leave

The only thing I can find to love tonight

Is how high the ceilings are in my apartment

The energy in here is stale

It hits before the door can close behind you

But it doesn't take much

When you're walking into emotions

As thick as fog

I wonder who else will stare at the ceiling here

And feel like I do

Once I'm gone from this place

Safe in its distance

But too high to touch

It's the little things now

That are left for me

Here

SOFTER

I hate you

For making me write about home

In a way

That made it seem

Real

To me

The air smells like donuts

But also kind of like you

And for a moment I wish you were the reason the morning smelled this way

Either way

I notice that it's sweet

And I return to myself, remembering sometimes things can be good

Just for me

Instead of for us

SOFTER

What will you miss about me

In the mornings?

I've gone too far too fast

To find a new home again

This one would be riddled with ghosts of you

That I'd see in every corner

A home is not one

I'll always feel nauseous in

SOFTER

If you find me in that deep cold stare

I've likely lost my way

Run your fingers through my hair

If you find me in that deep cold stare

And if it is too cold to bear

Please keep your fears at bay

If you find me in that deep cold stare

I've likely lost my way

Maybe it's not him

Or you

Maybe he's sweeter than both of you

SOFTER

Sweet slumber

How I long to greet you

With intentions other than

Forgetting being awake

Quiet sleep

How I wish to find you

At the side of a lover

I will get to call mine

(In time)

Gentle dream

How I want to keep you

At the front of my mind

For more than five minutes

Delicate rest

How I crave your nearness

After this darkest hour

Of my life

The same restless words repeat

Things can't be good for too long, child
You were right in your fears, child
It was all temporary, child
This is what suffering tastes like, child

Remember, child?

SOFTER

I get so angry

I could kick and

Kick

And kick

Until my feet are bleeding

That you think your pain was bigger

Since when do I care to compare hurt feelings

That is not something I usually want

To compete for

To the daughter I might have someday

You will be even more loved

Because of this

Your father will be strong in his kindness

Soft in his pain

Calm in his anger

And quiet in his thoughts

We will make you

To be all those things

And more

You'll be gentle

And sweet

And brave

And smart

But mostly,

You won't hurt people you love

Because this isn't for me anymore

It's for you

And you don't deserve a father like the one

I imagined you with

SOFTER

I didn't feel the wax spill

Or the oil

Pop

On my knees

Or

On my chest

I didn't feel

The whistle blow

Or the madness

Stop

In my knees

Or

In my chest

My body like a childhood home

I open the door

And welcome you

Not even summer was warm enough to replicate *us*

I feel like a drug addict

You intoxicate me

The type of love where you forget your name

I could walk blindly down the street to the sound of your love

And I know in an instant

It would end me

I am dizzy in it

You make me sick

At the edge of a cliff in the rain kind of love

Stomach aches on a Wednesday kind of love

Throw away all I've become kind of love

Release me,

Please;

Release me

SOFTER

I thought so,

I thought.

All I ever was

Was yours,

It's all I ever thought.

You can't tell me

You didn't make a home in my heart

Convince me

Your safe place

Wasn't found

Situated at the edge of my mind and soul

Where my wildflowers grow

The brightest

I was there when you built it

SOFTER

I've been sleeping in reverse

Waking up to the nightmares

Instead of lying with them

Staying asleep is more safe

Than anything I can do with my eyes open

Right now

There is no way to unravel the way our lives were mixed

You are so much like me

Now even my own belongings

Will look like

Yours

SOFTER

April 13th

No chalk on the sidewalk

No warmth of the sun

The walk by the water

Would have been rushed

Maybe we could have avoided it all

If only it rained

Two years ago today

I cut my fingernails to the skin

Trying to forget you

SOFTER

I don't feel like myself anymore

I talk to strangers

Trying to convince them I'm not one

I keep seeing myself in the mirror

I'm looking well

The men seem to agree

Somehow I wonder

If I'm glowing

Because I'm hollow

And all the light gets to just

Pour right in

I didn't know it would take three years to come down, but I'm on the floor

And my head is spinning

I've been ok, but only for five months

And that's only five months out of twenty-eight years

The last three tried to kill me

I'm finally tired

I'm finally aching

Nauseas

Tense

Weak

And quiet

And of course I don't want to be alone tonight

But it's so much safer when I am my own keeper

Three years is a long time to lie to yourself

Three years is a lot of time to waste

How long does it take to heal from this?

How long will I be here

On the floor?

SOFTER

I guess I liked the sour taste

You left on my tongue

Especially since tasting it

Was never up to me

It was like a treat

A special reward

For how well I had behaved

But maybe you've rotted now

Or maybe I've grown into a different taste

Because what used to be sour

Is bitter today

And I can't even remember why I didn't prefer

Sweet

To begin with

My home is

A ghost town

I can't find my shoes

The sink is empty

My bed is only warm

For a moment

The windows breathe life in

While I breathe

Out

I bet the walls stare at me

Like I'm lightning

Bright, fast, and terrifying

It's in these moments

I wonder who else's hearts have been broken

Hiding in plain sight

Right in front of me

SOFTER

So many things

Rest in winter

On my coldest days

I want to join the things

That rest

Remember how you hated the days

It snowed?

SOFTER

Not even the gentle kiss

Of the air

By the sea

Is helping

It feels like I have fallen completely into myself

In all the worst ways

Touch me

Don't you know flowers

Need nurturing?

SOFTER

It would be too much

I'd have to start liking palm trees

And decorate my house in pinks, yellow, and blues

Act like I'm someone different

Just to begin

Forgetting you

It feels like I'm running out of places to belong in this world

And the places I'd try

I am too tired for

Now

When the home you find

Becomes a home no longer

The earth

Somehow

Shrinks

SOFTER

I want to leave something somewhere

For so long

That it starts to get that sticky 'I've been here a while' dust on top

And I want to come back to it later

Looking down without a care that it hasn't moved

And notice

Just for a brief moment

That I've stayed in one place long enough

For that to happen

My pant leg is sticking out

Of my IKEA dresser

It's making me think about how impermanent home has always been for me

I wish I could turn rain into money

So I could just

Stay

SOFTER

The problem with running away

Is that each time I run

I don't get quite as far

And every new place I find

Needs to be

Even further

I want to forget I ever felt anything close to love

Or friendship

That sharing my life hadn't become my preferred way of living

Because then I could go on

And be alone

Need nothing

Need no one

And

I wouldn't be in danger anymore

I wouldn't need the seventeen deep breaths I've taken today just to get by

I would stop losing people

And

I might not be afraid of my birthday anymore

All would be still

And quiet–

And I could be wild

I could be wild and no one would care

I could be wild and no one would hurt me

I could be wild

And alone

And wild

And alone

And wild

And

Alone.

What's wrong with me

That I'd kiss your lips again

After you looked at my crying eyes

And winced?

Let your abuser hands

Hold my body

My one and only precious body

After you used the words

'Too much'

To describe my heart

What am I afraid of?

I'd rather go to the end of the world

Twice and back again

Than love you

One

More

Day

I want to lay down

Anywhere the earth can find me

Let my head kiss the floor

Let the ground feel the weight

Of the things on my mind

So just for a moment

I don't have to

SOFTER

New moon

The new moon fades into the old

I smoke this joint contemplating why I'm so fucked in the head

I've got my therapist convinced I'm a good person

She tells me that and points out how much of a mess I am in the same session

I wonder,

Can we really be both,

What do I pay you for?

One minute I think I'm the shit

One I'm contemplating the point of eating dinner because I'm not sure I'm worth the time spent on it

Nourishment blends into the same idea as love

What the fuck makes me think I should get any of that?

I'm sick of endings

Even the ones that set you free

I'm sick of it all

Why is it beautiful

To fall out of love

Along the way?

A narrative we've written for ourselves

Selfish and

Lazy

As if working for love

Was never

A priority

SOFTER

The sound of your voice,

The past,

Right now

Dripping off my tongue

Falling from my eyes

Beating in my heart

I just hope I can find you next to me

Tomorrow

And all over again

After that

My father taught me

I am delicate

That idea swirling in my head

Clear through to today

Like bugs around a light in June

I am delicate

I thought

I am fragile

I thought again

So I found men

And lay with them

They told me

(They still tell me)

I'm haunting

        I'm beautiful

                I'm intense

But birds sit on the backs of bulls

And the bulls forget they can fly

So I flew on home

SOFTER

I was in love

I was

And what I would give

To go back

And never be in love

So maybe now

I could be

My heart plays with me again

Such a sly thing that beats in my chest

Blood in, blood out

Dancing on the lines in the street

This is all that keeps me up at night

Promises of meadows green

Of lakes blue

Promises of me

Promises of you–

SOFTER

Pill packaged sunshine

Dry hot air from plastic machines

Heavy lotions

And clothes

And heart

My body needs extra care in the cold

But

I don't want it–

Just let me lay in the sun

Let the heat flush my cheeks

Let me forget the winter inside me

I want to release my pain

In a bliss

Of endless summer

A letter on November 22, 2020

I'm writing this poem from my bedroom in the West End in Portland, Maine (never quite felt a home like here)

Billie Eilish is playing

And it's been a warm November

I'm not sure if any of us (including me)

Really like Billie Eilish

Or if we are just lonely, longing to be liked, and hoping to stay young

These days

Anyway,

The world is on fire

And I have as many face masks as I do pairs of underwear

These days

I'm molding (as we all are)

Into something new

Something we didn't get to choose to experience

And I swear even sugar tastes sweeter

These days

I was in love recently

There's a wedding dress that I never wore in my closet

He still hopes I'll wear it someday, but I do my best not to be stupid

These days

SOFTER

I'll be 28 next Monday

I only have a fish for a pet

And I'm alone

But I have friends, health, and a warm home

What more could I really ask for? (people are dying)

These days

Sometimes I think about palm trees

And warm air in October

I wonder if I could just keep starting over

And over and over

But I think I'm too tired

These days

I just titled my second book

Assuming it's done being written

I wonder if anyone will care that my writing has gotten better

I walk around calling myself a poet before anything else

These days

I had sushi for dinner

I'm wearing a tourist sweatshirt from Rhode Island

I bought it the day I decided to move here

And I guess what I'm trying to say is

Things look so much different than I expected

These days

Stampede

Trample the dirty ones

They said

Take their breath

Joy could never live successfully

In every man

        (could it?)

Punish them for making love

Who are they to have found joy

When we haven't?

Shred it up

The paper to our rock

We just cannot have that

        (can we?)

SOFTER

This time

I am not where I started

This time

I am miles ahead

Almost like I could have another name

I imagine the woman I'd be

Loving someone

Better

I feel prettier

With you gone

My naked face feels better

Without your eyes

On it

And my stomach expanded

Both with air

And nourishment

Because since I escaped you

My body can finally relax

And since I escaped you

I feel the floor beneath my feet differently

And since I escaped you

I'm not afraid to jump in the ocean

I'm not afraid to be alone

I'm not afraid to

Keep

Living

Because when I use the word

> *Escape*

I am screaming it

I am so loud

Your mother flinched in her sleep last night

To the sound of me shouting,

> *Your son abused me*

And so,

Since I escaped you,

That's right

I'm not afraid to keep living

Because only dying could scare me

After loving you

Where loneliness haunts me

I will keep trying

Where failure finds me

I will keep trying

Where fear holds me

I will keep trying

Where love fails me

I will keep trying

SOFTER

Rolling tides

And eyes

Go forth like the wind

Be free from these lines

Leave your spot next to me

And untangled

You'll be

I like that you wouldn't have wanted

The loud and unforgiving woman

You made me

SOFTER

I will not allow myself to sink

Just because you are the ocean

And with you

Comes the depth

Of that truth

You haven't seen me yet, baby

I have a lot of practice

Rising above the tide

Did you forget

I am my home?

That once in a lifetime

Makes no sense until it does

Shakes you to the core

Effortless love

Will only find you

On one occasion

So,

Why are you worried when all your other loves

Haven't been quite enough?

That love,

The wild kind,

Is coming

But it's only coming

Once

SOFTER

I don't want to apologize for loving deeply

Or not at all

I just want to feel like I did

That time I jumped in the freezing ocean

Or ran in that soft warm field

Give me all

Or give me nothing

How could I ever want anything

In between

Gut Feelings

Can you hear them

Calling you, too?

It's the loudest sound

I've ever felt

SOFTER

I keep watching these blues

Wondering when they'll turn gold

I keep staying in my magic

Wondering when it will feel like magic

I keep being intense

Wondering when it will serve me

I keep looking forward

Wondering when I'll get tired

And look down

Trauma

A short thank you

To my shoulders

Feet

Hands

And hips

For holding onto what I didn't know my head couldn't handle

Since I was small

SOFTER

Let's go back

Before I used to notice how lucky I was for being able to watch birds fly parallel to the water

I didn't savor the sips of liquid I took onto my lips then

I let the days pass

As if endless

And even when I loved, I heartbreakingly admit,

It was fleeting

Always fleeting

But–

A love for the books wouldn't find me before I became selfless

And able to notice the ocean birds that fly so gracefully across the sea

So I sit

I rock on this floating dock

And I wish I could swim right now

And I wish I could swim

With you

I'm jealous of them

The ones who last in love

Wrinkled, stories behind their eyes

Who have chosen one another

Time and again

Will I ever know

What that

Feels like?

SOFTER

Mexico, the first time

The title of every poem

I'm trying to write

But can't

Let me be free in self love

Let me bear it like the teeth in my smile

Let me wrap myself in it like a blanket

Let me yell it

Whisper it

Sing songs about it

Tell stories of it

Become it

Live wholly alongside it

Go within in order to go without

Go without in order to go within

No matter the path

Rocks, sand, dirt, or otherwise

I walk steady on the road

To myself

SOFTER

This

Sideways

Backwards

Noise–

I can't stop finding myself entangled with those

Who just can't hear me

I swear my heart screams love

I swear it, I swear it, I swear it

But that doesn't mean I don't get angry

Get spiteful

Get tired

That doesn't mean I won't love who I love

Even when I didn't mean to

Just let me be loved,

I pray,

Just let me be loved

Can you hear me?

They continue insisting

I am such a force

That the word

Queen

Leaves their parted lips

In my direction

Even after I claim not to be

Both out loud

And in words

They say things like,

Look at your apartment

You're doing so well

I envy you

I wonder if they know how much money I put on plastic

Curious to hear what they'd think if I told them

I stay up all night

Just to be alone

After spending the whole day

Trying not to be

Do you think they'd still call me Queen

When they hear how much of a peasant

I am?

SOFTER

I don't want to walk up this empty dock alone

Only a piece of me will admit that anymore

The love left on my tongue

Still bitter

But I guess I should cherish that last remaining piece

That prefers company

Since I'm so close

To preferring

None

Choosing my words

In a powerful way

Has shown me the strength

Of language

How love can be spilled

From both the body

And the tongue

Still–

It's best to do both

At the same time

SOFTER

I know my wildflowers grow there

But it's a long walk to that corner of my mind

The seasons are harsh

And right now

It's winter in my head

But that doesn't mean they aren't coming

Because they are

And I think this season

They'll be

Bright lavender

I think I found my center here

A corner of this world

That holds me

Just a little tighter

I dance with ghosts on this beach

Mostly ghosts of myself

It feels like I come here to visit them

Tell them stories of where I am now

Somehow

No matter who can see me

I am alone here

In the very best way

Shedding

Shedding

Shedding

Another ghost

I'll dance with

When I return again

SOFTER

Your mother wants you to come home

Won't you come home?

Sweet girl

Can you tell

Your insides

Are magic?

I can see it from here

That's probably why

It's harder for you to enjoy

The outside

When there is a galaxy of light

Hiding

Inside you

SOFTER

I will not sit here useless

I will go on limitless

Men knock on my window

Try to quiet my reminders of loneliness at dusk

But I let them knock

I fall asleep to the sound of it

Comfort can't come from band-aid love

Not for me

23

Blind

24

Liar

25

Chained

26

Fooled

27

Softer

28

Free

I am the woman

To quiet the loudness

To soothe the worry

To calm the anger

I am the woman

Who chooses

And guides

And creates

Whatever it is

That needs molding

In my hands

It's clay

SOFTER

Wicked amongst the moon we fly

Thoughts turn quiet with a stare

From their tongues my lovers cry

As moonlight dances in my hair

All along my path so new

I walk with purpose

Without you

In fever dreams

Through hellish night

Lost somewhere

My soul takes flight

One beautiful piece of being alive

Is breathing in the air

Of each new place

You find

SOFTER

Even when she couldn't speak

She thought in poems

Like water through trees

After a morning storm

I fall into myself

The way rain

Falls into the earth

SOFTER

Any place

Or thing

That was once yours

Always will

Be

It's 9:28 p.m.

It's dark

My mother called me

She said she saw me reading poetry

She told me,

I wish I could have understood you then

As I understand you now

I was in Portsmouth

I was in my wedding shoes

My mother told me,

It was like watching the ocean

It's 9:28 p.m.

SOFTER

Don't fall in love with me

Don't–

I spit love on the street

I wash it down every drain in my house

I hide it like the crystals under my pillow

A girl like me has to do the falling

Let me love you

Let me–

I drink love like water

I bathe myself in it like it's sacred

I scream it like a song I've heard one hundred times

A girl like me has to do the falling

They place love at my feet. Safe love. The kind that feels like honey down your spine. And tastes just the same. And what do I do when they place it there? I crumble. I run. I make faces. I tell my friends I'm afraid. My grandmother's voice echoes in my head. *Find someone who'll take care of you.* And it sends me spinning. Spinning fishing poles that my dad set up for me every time they broke. Spinning tires on cars that my Papa showed me proudly in my brand new overalls. Spinning the studs in my ears my grandfather bought me from Italy. You see, I've always been loved gently by men until I wasn't. But once I wasn't, I started to like not being loved at all. Who wants to be the princess when you can be the queen? Being alone is much more predicable than loving men I might not love forever. Or men that might not love me forever. Or men I might love forever. Or men who might love me forever.

Who are we to mess with forever? Who am I to mess with love?

SOFTER

Falling from stars

Wild

Unimaginable –

Who might you

Be

Who might you

Become?

The tattoo on my back

Is about love

But before the love

Came the fucking

Does my face look like the face of a girl

Who's been fucked?

I can count the times a man has made love to me

Beads of sweat on his lip

Heart pours out

Into mine

My fingers in his hair

> *If I ever hold onto your hair,*
>
> *I might love you one day*

But I've been fucked

By many men

Even the men who have made love to me

I sit on beaches in Maine

Wondering

When someone will make love to me

And fuck me

At the same time

And part of me wonders

If it will be

You

SOFTER

Are your hands smart enough

To hold me

The way I need to be held?

I am water

To be contained

Takes strength of that which carries me

I might pour over you

Slip through your fingers

Freezing

Like ice–

Or I can be still

In a swirl of warmth

Beside you

Show me your hands

What am I to do

What am I to do

You remind me of him

You remind me of him

Kissing graves in this small town

I miss New York City

SOFTER

If you've caught yourself

A rare woman

I dare you

To keep her

I'm sorry for getting older

While we wait for one another, love

But I know you won't mind

In all your sweetness

I can see you, kind of

Dark hair

And that kind, tired look in your eyes

A look that will whisper to me

I'm the one

When I finally

Find you

SOFTER

Can you feel the sex

In my words

I begin them both

In the same way

Slowly

Until it can be anything

But that

If you could

Would you recall the moment

You were most loved

Or would you wait

Patiently

For when it happens to you

Next

SOFTER

I'm laughing under my breath

As I think about this

The ones who catch me

Don't know how often it is

I'm not able to be caught

I wonder if it's you

With the kind eyes I've imagined

So often

Keep whispering sweetness to me

And soon

I'll find out

SOFTER

Bright red

Luck

Crawled along my fingertips

On a cloudy Sunday in August

In my belly I knew

You were almost

Home

And probably Paris

On the raining streets of New Orleans

In the lobby of that Mexican resort

Bryant Park

Gas house beach

My Minnesota dock

Or

Quebec City at night

I suppose if you'd like to dance with me

I suppose there

I might

SOFTER

Over

Under

I always land

Upside down

In love

I think I could

        Slip

Jump

        Lean

Walk

        Run

Spin

Into love

A thousand times

I try

And I try

Again

But I can't seem to

        Fall

Ever since

You think

I'm pretty?

Wait until I split my head open

And start spilling the things

I only tell people I love

That's where you'll find yourself

Lost

A woman

Unlike others

Has a habit of becoming

Irresistible

SOFTER

Catching drops of honey in your hands

You realize my heart is sweet

And you grab on

Wash your hands now, baby

With your tongue

Taste every last piece of me

Surely, they must

I'd like to know how men are so spectacular at hiding their longing

Only from the lips of those who have accepted some severance

Would the words pour out,

I long for love

Don't you also crave that dense magic of safe and quiet slumber beside the love of a lifetime?

I'm not convinced that none of you dream in color

Of children and kissing in Paris cafes and simple mornings beside someone

Searching,

I will go on a skeptic

Somewhere, somehow

I know men must long for love

Surely,

They must

SOFTER

If I go home soon

You might notice

You're not the lover I'll keep

If I go home soon

That means I don't want to run in the summer streets with you

Indefinitely

When I'm in love

I want nothing more

Than to disappear into the fog together

So, if I go home soon

Forgive me,

You're not the lover I'll keep

I'm not the giggling type. I want to wake up to a man and not have to smile to seem happy. I want to look at him and smile with just my eyes and my heart. I want a quiet love. Strength is quiet. I hate it when all I can do is laugh. I bet you don't know that about me. Know that I don't always laugh around men I love. That I'd much prefer the silence of knowing we are still and one together. Save the laughing for the movies, for the jokes, for the dancing in the kitchen and for the times dinner comes out inedible. When I wake up, just let me look at you. Just let me look at you and wipe the dreams from my eyes and forget that I am anything but alive there in that moment with you; the quiet knowing causing not even the littlest smirk, because a love like that is more serious than many men find in a lifetime.

What's so funny about love anyway?

SOFTER

Lovely the way your skin

Brushes mine

As my words wash over you

None of them pretty

You listen anyway

Tempted by the love on my tongue

Speaking back each way you know how

Trying to save me

I pulled you right out of thin air, baby

Spooned you like ice cream

From the bowl I like to call

'Things I want'

Now you're just

There

Half melted

Swirling

Will this ever be more

Than a magic trick?

SOFTER

Things I'd only whisper to myself and my closest friends

It's ok if you don't want him

You don't have to take him into you

Just out of need

For human touch

It's safe to relax within yourself

Don't you know

Your own touch

Will be the sweetest

Until 'the one' comes along?

It's ok if you feel like you've already met him

And he's still calling you a witch

To describe the fact

That love is imminent

Together

And it's ok

That he's not the only one to have called you that this week –

It's ok

I don't want to walk in the middle of the road anymore

Even though it's a thrill,

You know,

To be the center of everything

In a place you shouldn't be

Danger behind and ahead of me

I like it though,

I want to feel dangerous

Do you think someone will want to feel that way

With me?

SOFTER

The perfect moment

When rain feels like

Kisses

Not pricks

Fog gently swirls

Curling my hair, as it does

My favorite sweater is wet

It doesn't matter

I am home and not home all the same

Maybe that's the feeling I've longed for

To be both lost

And found

Again—

Alone, alone, alone,

Beautifully

Maybe the color of the sky tonight

Is gently reminding me

The golden hour of my life

Is still ahead

SOFTER

I sit on these steps

This year of chaos

Finally coming to a close

No knocks on my window tonight

Just the sweet sway of things in the wind

And the sound of my own breath

In

Out

In

Out—

Goodnight, Portland

Isn't it lovely

That there are whales in the sea

And that I can compare

The size of my love

To them

SOFTER

Don't forget

Don't forget

Don't forget

You are something

You are

You are

You are

Strawberry moon

In the pink night

In the warm air

In the heat of flames

The dust settled

The flowers burned

The end arrived

And every moment since the orange fire burned under the pale strawberry moon

I have loved myself

I have kissed my skin

I have soothed my aches

I have met my fears and befriended them

Four full moons have passed since

Each turning the tides, many of which I swam in

An ending, as they do, bringing a new beginning

And so I'll meet you under the firth moon

And so I'll meet you under all the rest

Not your queen

I do bring a storm to every new place I go

The truth is I am both the storm and the calm after it

But even with the wind and the sideways rain

I am not your queen

I am not the queen of any place

I am not the queen of here

What you're feeling is energy of a thousand nights of sorrow

What you're feeling is electricity of holding every moment that brought me joy just one second longer than all the others

What you're feeling is the sparks flying right off of me

Because I've learned to live for the sake of being alive

And that makes quite a fire

Would a queen know how dirt tastes?

Would she have run from kings?

Would she kiss the lips of jokers?

I think she wouldn't

The only queen I'll be

Is my own

And perhaps of the man who will love me fully

So remember, next time

I am not your queen

But that I am

A storm

Remember me by the way I love

Remember me for chasing it when it wasn't mine

Remember me for wrapping myself in it when it was

Talk to me now as if love is something I care too much for

But think of me fondly

For love is what you'll think of

When you remember me

SOFTER

For John

What is love beyond words?

Past time

Past thoughts

Move through,

Love through

Face fear

Face truth

What is love beyond pain?

Fear not

Want not

Love through

Face fear

Face truth

I just want to sit

In the dark

In the rain

I can't tell if it's because of how beautiful it is

Or how beautiful I feel

Or how beautiful the sadness becomes

When you let it

But I want it

I want it to enclose me

I want to nurture my soul

Never let me go

I want it to be you

SOFTER

Rap songs on the road with my sister

Sometimes the world chooses where it will receive you

Like two hours north

At a waterfall

With my sister

Or eight-hundred miles from home

On a rooftop with strangers

At eighteen

Or here

In Portland, Maine

A city beside the sea

Isn't it magic

The way home becomes the people we are in a place

Instead of simply

The place itself?

I wait on love like I wait on riches

Hoping it will pay me off

Set me free

Keep me warm

I wait on love like I wait on miracles

Hoping it will change my mind

Soothe my worry

Bring me joy

I wait on love like I wait on you

Hoping it will end my endings

Offer me eternity

Forgive my past

I wait on love

SOFTER

It's not the men who'll love you most

All the love I fought for

At the backs of men

Wishing, quietly

All the acceptance I longed for

At the backs of strangers

Changing, silently

Being tired has a habit of releasing you

And so I laid down

Sleepless

Exhausted

The salty air being the only thing left to feel

Or to taste

And I stopped wishing quietly

And I stopped changing silently—

And I am so loved

Oh, I am *so* loved

Since that moment

So we come to be

Shoveling holes in the ground

In the dirt

Planting wishes that skip off of your fingertips

And lips

We talk to each other for a while

I tell you to water your wishes

With

I am

I am

I am

And you will find yourself there

Turning your head at the sound of it

And in the dust

In the swirls of wind in the dark

Don't forget

There are moons

And there are tides

Within you

SOFTER

I wish I could turn back time

Tell the girl I was

She would be so loved

So wanted

So embraced

That one summer

She wouldn't have enough time to be loved

As much

As she was

Collection

I know someday I'll sit and read these poems as a collection

And it will be like how I've felt this summer

Looking in the mirror

The sun has kissed me so well

That the bags under my eyes

And the paleness of my skin

Are both

Completely

Gone

And I'll remember these poems as the ones I wrote

The summer I was finally able to forget you

And I'll look up to the sky and I'll whisper,

Thank you,

And I'll look up to the sky and I'll cry,

I'm free

SOFTER

I am not the weak one

You are beautiful

And strong

Who made you to think

That isn't true?

Made you feel

The need to run

Endlessly

Away from anything

Resembling love?

Settle into it, sweet

Pull it toward you like a blanket

The warm love you deserve

To be enveloped in

Is yours

I used to meditate

Trying to put a face to the lover

I was missing

Tonight

As I sit I the pink light of the sun setting

The waves rolling lavender

And cotton candy

And deep blues my way

I finally

Quietly

Notice

I've been waiting for

Me

SOFTER

I find endlessness scattered around corners

Hints woven between dog-eared pages and letters with defined creases

Warm sun on naked shoulders

That makes freckles dance in July

Light brown, imperfect circles

And all around me

The air so much like bare skin

That the devil himself must fear such a place

And it is here

Beside the endless dreams that dance along pages in my freckled, sunshine sleep

That fear cannot find me

At the end of the day

In the dark

In the absence of time left

I find myself alone again

Luckily—

And I sink into the sheets

And I melt into my heart

And I notice how time feels different depending on how you spend it

And summer is gone

And it left with my sorrow on its back

SOFTER

I am the type of woman who needs both quiet and loud

One who will sling yellow dresses over chairs in strangers' homes

And admire how they look in foreign places

The type that finds masculine energy

Just as soft and beautiful

As feminine energy

And will surround myself in it like songbirds and quilts worn in by time

(But only with men who feel like home)

I am the type of woman to fall asleep so deeply

Yet awake to the sound of docks rocking in the darkness

I am a gentle woman

And a powerful one

A beautiful woman

And a harsh one

A young woman

And an aged one

What a privilege it is

To describe myself

This way

Where have you been, girl?

Sinking your own ship?

Rise

Rise

Rise

Have you forgotten

How you throw flames

When you are yourself?

More powerful

Than anything

Untouchable, really

Release from this blurry mess you fell into

Pave the life you crave

With your bare hands

And notice

While you do so

How great with strength

You always have been

We are not the weak ones

SOFTER

I search for peace

I walk along with those searching beside me

We dig holes in the ground looking for it

We find ourselves in each other's fears

Home feels like an absence of hate

Home feels like warm wind on your back

It's going to be ok if we stick together

It's going to be ok if we stick together

I found a new corner of the world to hold me

One much bigger than ones that held me before

Isn't it beautiful that there are pieces of this world

At every turn

That will whisper *home* in your ear

And so the soul speaks to the earth

And the earth speaks right back

It whispers,

Child, you belong

Child,

You belong

And just like that

You're safe

And just like that,

You're home

28

Love struck

And

Renewed

Karma whispers in my ear

Sends me floating into 28

Kisses me goodnight

I am loved unlike ever before

Handmade hope falls into my lap

The city I've built from

Fallen parts

And pieces

Circle,

Spin,

And glimmer

And the ocean rolls waves of hope

And the water kisses my fingertips and toes

And I greet this karmic year

And I can do nothing more than smile

I can do nothing more

Mermaid (because that's where I've found myself)

And the universe fought to free her

Only a loose grip

On this slippery soul

But it held tight

For it knew one day

She would arrive at the sea

And be one with her home

And it would become her

She would appear

More radiant than ever

True peace

Within and without her

And all other moments

She went unfree

Would forgive this one

For it was here

She was meant to land

At the sea

Softer

I am softer from the sand and water

I am softer from the time passing

I am softer from the sharp words on your tongue

I am softer from the days you terrified me

I am softer from it all

I bet you wish I grew harder, love

But I'm softer

I am so soft

The man who loves me next

Will never have felt anything like it

I bet he'll write you a thank you note

Describing all the ways you made me so delicate

Delicate to touch

Delicate to talk to

Delicate to be around

Delicate to taste

Delicate to love

Like velvet, but alive

So thank you,

I've always wanted to be softer

I didn't know monsters

Could make magic

reader,

may you never be led by fear
may you dance beneath stars in the sea
may the fire in your gut always warm you
and may you be eternally free

with love and gratitude,

maria k crawford

SOFTER

About the author

Maria K Crawford is a dreamer, a lover, and a romantic. She uses poetry as a way to reach not only her own heart, but the hearts of others. As she continues to live outside the lines, Maria is thrilled to welcome you into her world through words.

www.mariakcrawford.com

www.ingramcontent.com/pod-product-compliance
Lightning Source LLC
Chambersburg PA
CBHW031322160426
43196CB00007B/622